MW00323859

bush
PUBLISHING
& associates

AMAZING MARRIAGE

A 31 STEP DEVOTIONAL
TO A HEAVENLY MARRIAGE
USING THE KISS METHOD
(KEEP IT SIMPLE SAMUEL)

BY

SAMUEL MARTINEZ

COPYRIGHT

AMAZING MARRIAGE: A 31 Step Devotional to a Heavenly Marriage

ISBN: 978-1-7329751-1-8
Copyright © 2019 Pastor Samuel Martinez

Bush Publishing & Associates, LLC., books may be ordered everywhere and Amazon.com

For further information, please contact:
Bush Publishing & Associates www.bushpublishing.com

Printed in the United States of America.

TABLE OF CONTENTS

JUST ONE THING BRINGING THE GOSPEL (GRACE) INTO OUR MARRIAGES

With 31 steps, you may be thinking that the thought was to keep it simple. It is. Jesus told Martha that only ONE thing was needed (Luke 10:42). Just ONE thing. Think about this. The one thing that Mary did was spend time in His presence receiving from Jesus. The one thing we need is to come and receive from Jesus every day. Just giving you a list of principles to follow will not provide permanent change. Spend time with Jesus and His word, and you receive from Him.

Before I got married, people told me to "put God first in your marriage" or "make Jesus the foundation of your marriage." I never knew exactly what they meant. I have since discovered that making Jesus the foundation of our marriages means bringing in the gospel of Christ which is the grace of God into our marriages. Allow me to explain before we get into the steps. This introduction and steps one and two are the foundation of this book.

In studying Galatians 1:6-7, Paul tells the Galatians that they had departed from Him who had called them in the grace of Christ to a different gospel which Paul stated was not another gospel. Clearly, grace is the gospel. In Acts 20:24, this same Paul stated that he had been called to preach the gospel of the grace of God. In Romans 1:16, he further added that the gospel (grace) is the power of God unto salvation. The word in Greek for salvation is not just referring to being born again, but refers to healing, deliverance and preservation. Bring the gospel (grace) into your marriage, and you bring the power of God into it.

The Amplified Bible (AMPC) defines grace as the unearned and undeserved favor of God. I tell people all the time that God wants to do us favors every day, but we feel we have to earn everything He wants to give us. In the Christian's life we have available to us abundance of grace (Romans 5:17), great grace (Acts 4:33) and exceedingly abundant grace (1 Timothy 1:9). Furthermore, Ephesians 2:7 in the Amplified Bible (AMPC) talks of immeasurable, limitless and surpassing grace. If God wants to do us favors every day due to His grace, then He wants to do favors for us in our marriages.

Let's lean on His grace and not on our own self-efforts and knowledge to make things happen in our marriages. A good prayer to pray is "Lord I can't make things happen in my marriage but you can, so I trust you to work in it." Rest and listen to what He tells you to do. What He speaks in your heart and you apply is not you trying to make things happen but Spirit-led actions. Do what He tells you to do in Romans 5:17. Receive His grace, His unmerited and undeserved favor in your life every day. God will work in your marriage daily and not just when you do everything right.

To say it another way, grace is a person, Jesus (John 1:17). In Ephesians 5:25, husbands are told to love their wives "<u>as Christ loved the church and gave Himself for her</u>." That, my friends, is THE gospel and the power (Romans 1:16) that we must bring into our marriages. Jesus loves you. He gave Himself for you. This must be the cornerstone of your marriage; the knowledge of His love, His finished work, and that in Him we have been forgiven and made the righteousness of God in Christ. This further expounds on making Jesus the foundation of your marriage. My prayer is that you get a revelation of God's grace and love for you.

My desire is not just to give steps but unveil Jesus in our marriages. For example, in step three on understanding what biblical marriage is, we understand what God's intent for marriage has always been by looking at our Lord's unconditional, self-sacrificing giving love for us, the church. In step four on couples seeing each other as one, it is in the revelation that we are one with Jesus that we can see ourselves in our marriages as one. In step five on commitment, from understanding Jesus' commitment to us, as well as His grace and love, we are empowered to commit to one another. In chapter six on the importance of words, it is His words of grace and love that have transformed us that we can now give to one another in marriage. I could go on and on.

I know marriage can be very challenging, but only because we do not seek help from the Author of marriage, our Heavenly Father, and bring Jesus into our marriages. As a result, discouragement, selfishness and self-centeredness enter. Marriage was not intended by God to be so hard.

Read this book one chapter per day. If you decide to read it all in one sitting, go through it later one chapter at a time, slowly. Most chapters are intentionally short. In our fast-paced world, most couples will not sit and read a lengthy book on marriage. Hopefully, you, my reader, will take the time to read and meditate on the truths in this book and read the recommended Bible verses. When you go through all thirty-one chapters, I encourage you to go through them again periodically to keep the marriage brimming. Again, do not skip steps one and two. Without them, you cannot bring the gospel of grace or God's favor, Jesus, into our marriages.

God is on your side and understands that marriage can be the closest thing to heaven and at the same time life's greatest challenge. That is why He provided the Bible, the greatest (and simplest) instructional manual on marriage. Rest assured that you are not alone in making your marriage work. Be blessed as you read and keep it simple.

GET A REVELATION THAT GOD LOVES YOU

Nothing makes the Christian life a success like the revelation of God's love for you and a revelation of your righteousness before God. God loves you unconditionally and totally. Marriage works best when both spouses have a revelation of how much God loves them. God is not as concerned that you realize that He loves the world as He is desirous that you get a revelation that He loves YOU specifically. He wants you to believe that He loves you (1 John 4:16). I have said many times that Christianity is not about how much we should love God but about getting a revelation of how much God loves us. When we receive His love, then we can with the love with which He loves us, love Him and love our spouse.

When I tell others that God loves them, some people tell me that God loves everyone. Then I add that is not what I told them. My friend, nothing will make marriage, and everything work in our lives like the revelation that God, the God of Abraham, Isaac and Jacob, the Father of the

Lord Jesus Christ loves you and Jesus loves you. After all, He died for you even when you wanted nothing to do with Him (Romans 5:8).

Here is the bottom line. You cannot give to your spouse what you do not have. If you do not have a revelation of how much God loves you, then you have nothing with which to love your wife or husband. On the contrary, you will be demanding love from the other instead of giving love. Remember that the Great Commandment of Jesus is to love one another as He loves us.

Go to the Scriptures and read verses on the love of God for you and meditate on them daily. He loves you. The Bible was not written to prove the existence of God, but to reveal His nature. He does not have love; He IS love. Let's keep it simple. Read primarily the New Testament. In the Old Testament, Jesus had not yet come to pay for all our sins. Since He has come, God is not holding our sins against us (2 Corinthians 5:19). We are right before Him because we have become the very righteousness of God in Christ (2 Corinthians 5:21).

I know some people read the Old Testament and see only the anger of God. Actually, His love is throughout the Old Testament, but many miss it. Even the Old Testament states that a time would come when God would no longer be angry with us (Isaiah 54:9). That time is now because Jesus took all the judgment for our sins.

In Matthew 3:17, when Jesus was baptized His Father stated, "This is my beloved Son in whom I am well pleased." My friends, if Jesus is your Lord and Savior, you are pleasing to God and His beloved. Ephesians 1:6 indicates that we are IN the Beloved. If we are in the Beloved, then we are beloved. As He is so are, we in this world (1 John 4:17). Furthermore, we are His body-the body of the Beloved.

Read the verses at the bottom until you have a revelation of how important you are to God. And thank Him every day for loving you until it becomes real in you. God is for you (Rom. 8:31). He is on your side (Psalm 118:6), and He is in you (1 John 4:4). Hold on to the dream you have for your marriage. He will grant it to you because He loves you and not because you have done everything exactly right. When you make mistakes in your marriage, remember that you are still the righteousness of God in Christ and have His favor on your side. He is the God of all grace (1 Peter 5:10). Receive His love daily (especially when you do not feel loved), receive His grace and receive daily that you are the righteousness of God in Christ. Receive and keep it simple.

Key Verses: John 17:23, John 15:9, Jeremiah 31:3, 1 John 4:9-19, Ephesians 1:6, Ephesians 3:16-19

KNOW THE REALITY OF YOUR COMPLETION IN CHRIST

Let me reiterate, nothing makes the Christian life work more than a revelation of how much God loves you and a revelation of our righteousness before God. So many times, in our pop culture we use expressions that most of us do not know what they mean. They may sound good, so we accept them at face value. Take, for example, the expression, "I found my soulmate." Another one is to tell your new-found love "you complete me." I have no idea what either expression means, but I can tell you something very important. No one but Jesus can complete you. No one but Jesus is big enough to complete you. As much as I love my wife of over 48 years, she <u>compliments</u> me but cannot <u>complete</u> me.

We cannot and should not look to another person to complete us, make us feel good about ourselves or even make us feel loved. I know my wife loves me and I feel her love. But I quit looking to her to feel good about myself and to feel loved. I am to love <u>her,</u> not look to her to make me feel loved. Do not misunderstand me. At times, I go to her and tell her I need a hug. She gives me one willingly. However, on another day she may be going through her own issues and is not emotionally present. I can then pout or go get an embrace from God. What I am talking about is not being dependent on your spouse to make you feel good about yourself or feel loved.

Believe God loves you. This completes you. Ultimately, only He can fill all your love needs. You have heard husbands refer to their wives as their better half. What nonsense. Marriage is not two halves coming together. It is two whole people coming together who have made Jesus the Lord of their lives and obtained a revelation of how much God loves them. The best thing two people can do who are planning on getting married is to make Jesus Lord of their lives and get a revelation of how much God loves them. The same thing applies to two people already married.

To grow in the reality of our completion in Christ, we must receive His love for us every day and hear messages on our completion in Christ and who we are in Him. Refuse to look to others for your completion. As far as the Father is concerned, we are already complete in Jesus. Jesus is our wisdom, righteousness, sanctification and redemption (1 Corinthians 1:30). As He is so are, we in this world (1 John 4:17). In Him, we are washed, sanctified and justified (1 Corinthians 6:11). This is our completion, so keep it simple like the children's song. Jesus loves me this I know for the Bible tells me so.

Key verse: Colossians 2:10, and you are complete in Him, who is the head of all principality and power.

UNDERSTANDING WHAT BIBLICAL MARRIAGE IS

Whing God stated in Genesis chapter two that it was not good for man to be alone, He was not stating that man was lonely. If this had been the case, He would not have called His finest creation, man, "very good." God was simply stating that man needed another being like himself. Otherwise, man would forever only be concerned for himself. God brought Eve to Adam not just because men need a lot of help but so that Adam would develop the divine nature of love that He had placed in him. With the arrival of Eve, Adam was not just thinking of himself anymore.

Marriage was God's idea from the beginning. His purpose in marriage was not just to create the Human Race but as a picture of the love relationship between Jesus and the church, His body. As we get a revelation of this love relationship (which Paul in Ephesians chapter 5 called a mystery), we begin to love like God. We should enter marriage not for what the other can do for us but committed to doing all we can for the other. <u>Biblical marriage is the process of the development of the love of God and the elimination of all selfishness and self-centeredness.</u> At least it should be.

We marry because we want to commit ourselves to the other for the rest of our lives, to do anything and everything to make heaven on earth for the other. We commit to forsake all others and decide to dedicate ourselves to do all we can for our loved one simply because we love them. We start out well but when the other does not reciprocate, we forget why we got married. But in reality, what does this have to do with our commitment?

Marriage is telling my fiancé, "I love you so much, I am forsaking all others and committing myself to bring heaven to earth for you. I am committed to doing all I can to help you become all God has called you to be and accomplish on earth." This is death to selfishness and self–centeredness. Did not Jesus say that he that would lose his life would find it? Lose your selfish self-interests in marriage, lose the love of God in it and you will find heaven on earth. This is Biblical marriage in its simplest form. Hard? Yes, but only if we try to do all this on our own. Remember the simple prayer in the introduction (Lord, I can't make it happen, but you can, so I trust you to work in my marriage) and that grace is available to you, so keep it simple.

Key verse: Genesis 2:24, Therefore a man shall leave his father and mother and be joined to his wife, and they shall become one flesh.

WE ARE ONE

L et me continue with understanding what Biblical marriage is. Marriage is the joining of two spirits into one. The problem in marriage is that we do not see ourselves as one. When you said, "I do," most people do not believe or understand that the two became one. Now, most people may say that they already know this, but I question this. If we truly understood that we are one not just legally but more importantly spiritually would we argue about MY needs? Would not our mindset be OUR needs or more importantly the other person's needs? Marriage is not my needs or her needs but the other person's needs period. That is, as a husband what I should have on my mind is her needs. My wife, of course, should have my needs on her mind but, whether she does or not, on my mind is one thing - her needs, because her needs are OUR needs. Get it? What she needs I need. When I am meeting her needs, I am meeting mine because we are one.

This is what Paul had in mind in Ephesians chapter 5 when he told husbands to love their wives as their own bodies. He stated that the husband who loves his wife loves himself. How simple can this be? In meeting her needs, my needs are met because her needs are OUR needs. Remember that Solomon stated that a merciful man does good to himself (Proverbs 11:17). This operates in marriage more than in any other area.

We are one in marriage. The minute we were born again we became one spirit with Jesus (1 Corinthians 6:17). The revelation knowledge of who we are in Him and He in us impacts our marriage, parenting and all areas of our life. 2 Corinthians 5:17 and so many other verses that point to us being in Him should further help us see ourselves as one with Jesus. Being one with Him, we have His nature, His life and ability in us. We need an understanding of all these to triumph in marriage. According to John 17:21-23, it is in knowing we are one in Jesus and the Father that oneness in the body of Christ (and in marriages) occurs.

Along these lines, remember the Emmaus incident in which Jesus revealed Himself in the scriptures to Cleopas and probably his wife. As Jesus expounded on Himself, the scripture states that the two disciples stated, "Did not our heart (singular) burn within us." The implication is clear that the more we focus on Jesus and the scriptures and focus and talk about Jesus the more oneness occurs in our marriages. This is in line with the first three chapters of this book. As both husband and wife see Jesus in the Word and obtain a revelation of His love for them, oneness occurs. We must not forget this truth even as we venture into the additional chapters in this book. What I must do as a husband and my wife must do in the marriage is secondary to understanding all Jesus has done for us. The revelation of what Jesus has done is grace, and grace empowers both husband and wife. When conflicts or hurts occur, have communion. In fact, have communion regularly. This brings unity in a marriage like very few things can.

When we expressed our marriage vows, God honored our words of faith and love and brought a miraculous union of two spirits. Therefore, when we attack one another, we are attacking ourselves. When we love the other and put them first, we simply love ourselves. Actually, if both my wife and I are one with Jesus, to love her is to love Jesus. How cool is this? Keep it simple.

Confession: I thank You, Father, that You have made my wife (or husband) and me one.

COMMITMENT

Commitment, not love, makes marriage work. Of course, my commitment must be first of all to the Lord and His Word. The best Christian makes the best spouse. When I am committed to doing whatever God tells me in ALL areas of my life, I will do what He tells me in my marriage. Remember that Jesus stated that He would never leave us nor forsake us. He is totally committed to us. Knowing this helps me with my commitment to my spouse. We have all experienced being forsaken and rejected but He never will. His love for us does not go up or down based on our behavior. Glory to God!

When I state to couples that commitment not love makes marriage work, I get their attention. It is the **feelings** of love that I am referring to. What happens when the feelings of love vanish? Most begin to question if they were really in love. This is a useless exercise. When and if the feelings of love vanish, what will make marriage last and flourish is remembering that I made a promise and will now DO love even if I do not FEEL love. When I commit to this, I resurrect the feelings of love. One of the greatest things I have learned about marriage is that words and actions keep feelings alive. We can say it this way- that words and actions keep the commitment firm and passion alive.

However, many times feelings take over because we have been trained to give them so much attention and value. But really what do feelings have to do with this? A great man once stated that most people do not do what is right, but only what feels right. The ability to have and express feelings is God-given, but some emotions and feelings are not ordained by God. Furthermore, being led by our feelings is not God-given.

As children, we learned quickly that some things feel enjoyable and some do not. But it is time to grow up. Marriage grows us up. My friend do what is right because it is right whether you feel like it or not. This makes marriage work. God will honor your actions, and the feelings will return. However, ultimately refuse to base your marriage on feelings, but on the rock of what is right. Base it on commitment. Paul stated that discipline is never enjoyable, but we do enjoy the results of it later (Hebrews 12:11).

Remember that in the marriage ceremony we promised to love no matter what. The first reason we did this was to remind ourselves of Jesus' commitment to us (Hebrews 13:5-6). The second reason we did this was so that when we did not have the desire or feelings to do for the other, the commitment would take over. Reminding ourselves of Jesus' commitment to us will strengthen us to let the commitment to our spouse take over and keep the marriage strong. Trust me; your commitment will resurrect feelings and passion like never before if you stay with it. Keep it simple.

Key Verse: Psalm 15:1 and 4b, Lord who may abide in Your tabernacle? He who swears to his own hurt and does not change.

THE IMPORTANCE OF WORDS

Words are the most powerful things in the universe. It was with words that God made all things. It was with words that God made man. In John 1:3 we learn that all things were made by the Word of God. In Hebrews 1:3 we learn that God's Word sustains all things. Your marriage is sustained by words. Only speak words of faith and love over your marriage. Only speak words of faith and love to one another. When you notice the passion leaving your marriage, on purpose speak to your spouse words such as "I love you, you are important to me, and I am glad I married you."

Generally, women desire words of affection daily, and men words of praise. This leads me into discussing the major need of wives, which is affection. We know this not because of a myriad amount of psychological studies in the last few decades, but because the scriptures state this in Ephesians chapter 5.

Though affection can be expressed in more than just words, words of affection are a priority for women. However, as much as women like to hear words such as what I just mentioned above, men like to hear, "That was a good job. You did well in that endeavor," or even, "You can do it." Nothing motivates a man more than the words of a woman.

But am I not being hypocritical to say words I do not even feel like saying? No, because you are <u>on purpose</u> releasing the force of love which has been shed abroad in your heart (Romans 5:5). It just became buried under resentments or simply the numerous mundane tasks of life. However, your spirit is committed to love your spouse forever. It is simply your flesh that is struggling with it.

When you say the words of faith and love on purpose, you are releasing the force of love in your born-again spirit. You are releasing love which is God. Then the passion shows up again. Do not wait to <u>feel</u> love before <u>expressing</u> it. This is one sure way to kill your marriage or at the least the passion in it. I will reiterate what I shared in the introduction that I am talking about relying on the grace of God. I am not telling couples as the comic strip used to say to, "Grin and Bear it" or as others have stated, "Fake it till you make it." Rely on the grace of God to help you express love even when you do not feel it.

Keep the words of faith and love flowing. Do not stop the flow. As I stated in the previous chapter, words keep feelings alive. You can see now how criticism will do the opposite. Avoid words that you do not mean. They can set destructive forces in motion in your marriage. God framed the worlds through words (Hebrews 11:3), and you will create heaven on earth in your marriage through words. Therefore, only speak what you desire to come to pass in your marriage. More on this later, so keep it simple.

Key verse: Proverbs 18:21, Death and life are in the power of the tongue, and those who love it will eat its fruit.

FIND OUT WHAT LOVE IS
TO YOUR SPOUSE

Ask one another, "Honey tell me what is love to you; what can I do to make you feel loved?" Keep the answers positive. Do not say things such as, "well when you pick up your dirty clothes after your shower, because I am tired of picking up your stuff." Just express that love to you is when he picks up after himself. Of course, the receiving spouse needs to keep it positive as well. Never say, "Are you trying to say I <u>never</u> pick up my dirty laundry?" And both remember that tones are very important in your answers.

The more specific you are, the better. A statement such as "that you respect me more or help around the house" is not specific enough. How about things such as "when I get home, and you give me a hug" or "when you help me clean the kitchen." I can also add, "when you listen completely" instead of saying "when you do not interrupt me."

Set some quiet time aside and ask the big question, "Honey, tell me what love is to you." No philosophical or even theological answers are permitted. What is important is to share what makes you feel loved. Then listen and take notes. NEVER assume your spouse knows and never demand that they know if you have not communicated clearly to them what love is to you.

When I got married, I assumed that my wife would feel loved by my cleaning the kitchen, doing the laundry, and vacuuming the house. This was how my mother felt loved, so I assumed that was how my wife would feel loved. Later, I discovered she enjoyed my help around the house, but there were other more important things that made her feel loved. So never assume. And remember to keep asking this question through the years because what makes your spouse feel loved will change. Additionally, your spouse may need to remind you of something that you used to do and have let slip.

If you have stated what love is to you, and you feel that your spouse simply did not listen or care, keep reading. Maybe you need to ask the Holy Spirit to teach you how to better communicate your needs to your spouse. Let me add here to state, not nag. Tell one another, "Honey, I feel loved when you do such and such," and leave it there. Do not keep bringing it up again and again in a complaining way. Of course, gentle reminders are always good. Trust the Holy Spirit to bring it to their remembrance. When your spouse does something to make you feel loved, tell them.

And finally, remember that this exercise is not primarily for your spouse to get to know <u>your</u> needs, but for you to get to know <u>theirs.</u> However, you should not feel guilty about letting your spouse know what love is to you; so keep it simple.

Key verses: Isaiah 5:13, Therefore my people have gone into captivity, because they have no knowledge; Proverbs 4:7... In all your getting, get understanding.

DON'T TRY TO CHANGE THE OTHER - LET GOD CHANGE YOU

Most couples go to counseling hoping that the other will change. But let me give you a secret. You cannot change another. Actually, if you have been married more than two days, you should already know this by now. So why do we keep trying to change the other? Because if I work on changing you, I do not have to change me. Even in abusive relationships such as where domestic violence exists, the abused one needs to change, by leaving.

But what if you definitely know your spouse is wrong? Well, pray that the eyes of their understanding will be opened, and then allow God to change <u>you</u>. But I am not the one needing to change, you might state. But you still need to change so that the other's actions will no longer bother you. This is the change I am talking about. This is liberating. My spouse (as an example) may still talk too much at parties, but I am no longer bothered by that. I have changed.

Let me explain what I mean by letting God change you. For years through my own self-effort, I worked hard on changing me. It brought little change and a lot of frustration. When I received the love of God and His grace, and the reality of my righteousness in Christ, change was effortless. This is how we allow God to change us. When something about my spouse bothers me, I can ask God for His help so that it will not bother me. This does not mean I may not talk to my spouse about it. However, as I approach my spouse, my communication will be healthier since I am not bothered any longer.

Again, I am not talking about relationships where abuse is occurring be it physical, drug-related, or emotional abuse. But even in these relationships, many times the victims enter into unhealthy relationships with the abusers, thinking they can change them. If an alcoholic or drug abuser refuses to get help, the victim should change by leaving. But my point is that even in normal relationships (whatever normal is), we spend so much energy getting the other to change that resentments build up. I like to tell couples that when they push someone in marriage (to change), the other usually pushes back.

Another area of change is this. Be willing to examine yourself in the event that you may be doing something to fuel the actions that bother you in the other. This is true unconditional love. You change recognizing that your behavior was bringing out negative behavior in the other. A key point in marriage is that whenever one spouse changes it eventually brings out a change in the other.

A word of caution. Do not take this step and tell your spouse, "See you are supposed to change and not nag at me to change," especially when you know there is an area you need to change. In another step, I will address avoiding doing things that frustrate one another. Take all the steps in this book for your benefit, not to throw them at the other, and keep it simple.

Key verse: 2 Corinthians 13:5, Examine yourselves as to whether you are in the faith.

HONOR

This could actually be step one because of its importance and due to the fact that it makes all the other steps work much more easily. The word for honor in the Bible (Old Testament) means to be heavy or weighty. In essence, it means to place a high value on something or someone. You can see why this is so important. If you do not place high value on your spouse, you will not place high value on your marriage. From this, you will not place high value on his or her needs. It will not be important what love is to them. You will not listen attentively to them, nor concern yourself much with the other steps.

Honor is a command from the Lord. It is not based on what the other does for me but on their position. Consider parents. God tells us to honor them period. We may have had great parents or poor parents, but regardless we are commanded to honor. The same works for political leaders. You may not even like them, but should not speak dishonorably of them, and address them respectfully by their title.

When I place high value on my spouse, I never speak dishonorably of them especially joking of them in the presence of others. I honor their opinions and feelings even if I disagree with them. I do not correct them in public even if (as an example) the story they are relating to friends did not take place on a Thursday but on a Friday. Most of the time it really matters little. Honor listens. Honor addresses our spouse respectfully. Avoid pet names if your spouse does not like them. What is wrong with calling one another sweetheart or honey? Honor is being courteous, but that is another chapter.

Honor is a decision. It starts there and in the mind. When I determine only to think good thoughts of my spouse, I can honor more easily. Even knowing the areas where my spouse is not quite perfect, I can still make a decision to honor. Never let the devil change your mental picture of your spouse. If it changes it will be difficult to honor. To realize that your spouse is not perfect and still decide to maintain a good mental picture of them is honorable. Remember if your spouse is not perfect, neither are you. Smile, couples.

And above all, remember that God has honored you and me. He has crowned us with His glory and honor (Psalm 8), seated us with our Lord Jesus in heavenly places (Ephesians chapter 2), and accepted us in the Beloved One (Ephesians 1:6). Knowing how He has honored us empowers us to honor others. Constantly ask yourself in your marriage, "What is the most honorable thing to do in this situation?" Honor one another. God stated that He would honor those who honor Him, and to honor others (especially your spouse) is to honor Him. In other words, I honor my wife since it honors Jesus who has honored me by all He has done for me and continues to do. I love you, Jesus. Keep it simple.

Key verse: 1 Peter 2:17, Honor all people.

EXPRESS, DO NOT ATTACK

Now that we have covered honor, this should be easier to do. When I place a high value on the other, I will express what I am feeling but never attack their character or person. Actually, this is one of the simplest steps in this book. I will express what I am feeling by starting my statements with the words "I am feeling such and such." This is the opposite of starting my statements with "you are this" or "you are that." The problem with the latter approach is that the walls tend to go up immediately when attacked. Communication will go downhill from there. Even a statement such as "the lights were left on" is better than "YOU left the lights on."

In other words, express what you are feeling rather than blast the other person. For example, if husband is always late for dinner and never calls, the wife should express what she is feeling rather than attack husband as being insensitive. Maybe he simply has let too much work get in the way. However, he still needs to know what she is feeling. There is a greater chance that he will understand if she expresses rather than attacks.

Here is a big tip. Never approach your spouse until you are clear on what you are feeling. In the example above, hopefully, the wife will express feeling taken for granted and unappreciated rather than just expressing her anger and attacking him for only thinking of himself. Also, make sure that you have calmed down as much as you can because even your expressing statements will sound accusatory.

Furthermore, your motive in approaching your spouse should be to bring restoration to the relationship. Your motive is not necessarily so that they will feel bad about what they have done or for them to even say that they are sorry. Lessening your expectations is good here. It is good if they do apologize. But even if they don't just the fact, they have listened to you is good. In many marriages, we expect too much when we approach our spouse. If they do not feel bad or apologize, we think the confrontation was useless. Not at all. As you shared your feelings respectfully, trust God that the Holy Spirit will remind them of what you shared. And if the Holy Spirit never reminds them about what you shared maybe it was never important to begin with. Here is where trusting God comes in.

Along these lines, I always recommend to couples in premarital counseling to write out their conflict resolution rules before they marry. By this, I mean to have them agree beforehand what they agree to do or not do when a disagreement occurs after they marry. I advise them to come up with their own rules but encourage them to write such things as have been discussed above along with no name calling, avoiding the statements such as you <u>always</u> do such and such, and you <u>never</u> listen, or basically any statements that are attacking. Additionally, agreeing not to shut down when a serious issue has to be discussed is good as well. Some couples have agreed not to drop a discussion until some understanding occurs (not always easy). Others have agreed to take a break when the discussion is becoming intense and pick it up later. Couples have to do whatever works for them.

Most people believe that couples with healthy marriages never argue. This is a myth. The difference in couples with healthy marriages is that they have learned to bring issues up that need to be discussed without attacking. They also have learned (as discussed above) to take timeouts when the discussion is getting heated. Remember the steps in this book such as honor and listening. This takes practice, so ask the Lord to help you in this and all areas and keep it simple.

Key verses: Proverbs 15:1, A soft answer turns away wrath, but a harsh word stirs up anger. Proverbs 16:21b and 24, … and sweetness of the lips increases learning. Pleasant words are like a honeycomb.

MAJOR ON THE MAJORS

I f you have been married more than one day you know that there is a tendency in all of us to become picky over minor issues. Yes, I know it is frustrating when the lights are left on in the bathroom, but is it worth the time and effort it will take to have an argument over this? Even more important are the resentments that build up over the constant nitpicking. A spouse can become stubborn about listening to a complaint or concern when a major issue <u>does</u> need to be discussed.

So, what do we do? Well, ask yourself the question. Is this issue worth getting into an argument over? Why not save your time and energy for when you definitely need to discuss an issue? Now, I am not stating just to ignore the issue you are bothered about or be in denial about it. What we need to do is work out the issue in our own mind. After all, <u>we</u> are the ones with the problem, not the other. I purposely ask the above-noted question and may even add the additional question, "Will my relationship be better off by my bringing this up now?" Please do not take this as a license for abuse or the like. I am talking about my spouse cutting the steak with the regular knife rather than the steak knife even when they have been told to use the proper knife several times.

Another example is the toothpaste. One spouse may believe it is a sin (I know I am exaggerating a bit to prove a point) not to roll the toothpaste, another could care less. Therefore, get two rolls of toothpaste since this is a minor (trust me it is) issue. Major on the majors and let the minors stay minor.

A word of caution, however. If your spouse is upset about a matter, never upset them further by sermonizing that the issue that is upsetting them is a minor issue for you. Basically, if it is important to my spouse, it will be important to me. Hope you see the balance here. Keep smiling and keep it simple.

Key verse: Song of Solomon 2:15, Catch us the foxes, the little foxes that spoil the vines, ...

MEN, YOU HAVE A GOOD THING

Proverbs 18:22 states that he who finds a wife finds a good thing. It does not state that he who finds a girlfriend or a fiancé, but he that finds a wife. Wives are in it for the long haul. A girlfriend may or may not be a keeper, and a fiancé may want a prenuptial agreement. But a wife is committed.

Men remember a great truth - perception creates reality. If you perceive your wife as a good thing, she most likely will become a good thing AND do good things for you. I could add that she is probably doing good things already. The Bible teaches us that women are helpers; the same word that the New Testament uses to describe the work and nature of the Holy Spirit (John 14:26). Men let's see the connection. Wives are helpers sent from our Heavenly Father who loves us, men. Why would God send me something that would harm me? So, if God has blessed men with women, thank God for them and treat them as gifts from God!

A major tactic of the devil that I have told many couples about is his plan to change the inner picture (which determines my attitude) that we have of our spouse. When that mental picture changes, even the good they do is not seen and the little things we do not like become major issues. Little by little another person begins to look more attractive. You can see how affairs start in our thought patterns.

I do not address affairs directly in this book because every chapter addresses the issue of preventing affairs. Someone once said that in the Christian life if we work on the "do's" the "do not's" will take care of themselves. Work on honoring one another, seeing value in one another and the other steps in this book and, in essence, you are building an affair-proof marriage without effort. I do not have to work on not committing adultery (old covenant) when my priority is to love my wife every day as Christ loves me (new covenant).

Therefore, husbands, refuse to let the devil change the picture you have of your wife. (This works for wives also). Couples cast down any negative thoughts the devil brings to you concerning your spouse (2 Corinthians 10:5). Men, remember the picture you had of her before you married? Yes, I know it was a bit unrealistic. But now you can have a more mature mental picture. Knowing that she is not perfect but still maintaining the inner picture that she is a good thing will create greater peace in the home.

Furthermore, men, you will not misunderstand her when she corrects you about something. She is a good thing and is trying to do you good. Men let her do her job. If nothing else she is a good thing because she was willing to commit for life. Remember Proverbs 31:12 states that your wife will do you good and not evil all the days of her life. Give her permission to do so.

And finally, since I am talking to men in this chapter, it is important men that we refuse to blame our wives for problems that come up in the marriage. Ok, maybe she had a part to play in a particular issue or problem, but you probably did too. The first one to truly accept responsibility is the strong one. This is part of being the head of the union. The head accepts responsibility. This is the high road. This is the loving way which releases the force of love and God Himself into our marriage.

Men are probably thinking that they will accept responsibility for their part hoping the wife will then accept responsibility for her part. No, men, accept responsibility period. If she comes around later and accepts her part, fine. If she doesn't, God will reward you for walking in love. Yes, I know this takes faith and grace. Trust God. Our Heavenly Father is on your side, men. He is cheering you on, so keep it simple.

Confession: Father, thank you for my wife. She will do me good all the days of my life. She is a good thing.

UNDERSTANDING SUBMISSION

Perhaps few things in the Bible are more misunderstood than submission. To begin with, in the book of Ephesians (5:21-24), where Paul discusses submission, he starts by admonishing all believers to submit to one another. Hence, husbands are to submit to their wives as wives are to submit to their husbands.

Yes, I know Paul seems to give more attention to the issue of wives submitting to husbands. However, a review of Ephesians 5:21-33 shows that the husband is given the major responsibility which is to love his wife as Christ loves the church. I believe that any woman will submit to a husband who loves her as Jesus does.

Submission is not dominance. Submission is only submission when it is given voluntarily, not demanded forcefully. Submission is an attitude of the heart and not the control of another. In martial arts (MMA), submission is <u>forcing</u> your adversary to give up by force. Biblically, submission is <u>given</u> from the heart as when we submit to Jesus. In essence, submission is to honor. Husbands, loving your wife as Christ loves the church is you submitting to her but more importantly, to Jesus.

Ephesians 5:33 shows the major need of the husband which is to be respected and honored. Hopefully, we can agree that keeping things in context a woman submits to the husband when she respects him. This, in my opinion, is the man's major need – to be respected. But aside from this being a man's major need, it is the command of scripture. As stated in the last chapter to men, perception creates reality. As a woman respects her husband, God will reward the fact that she is honoring His Word by doing work in her husband. In the last chapter, I told the men that our Heavenly Father is on their side. Wives, He is on your side as well.

Women, even when you have to confront him or correct him, do it with this in mind that you have been commanded by God to respect. We can see a great truth here that the husband needs to see his wife as a good thing and the wife needs to treat him with respect. And yes, respect goes both ways.

Men need to understand that the man being the head does not mean never listening to her input. Head is not dictator. Head means he should be hearing from God how to honor his wife, how she is doing, what she needs from him and what the children need from him. And men, your wives are your equal. In Genesis before the fall, God's empowerment to be fruitful, subdue and have dominion (Genesis 1:28) was to both of them. Furthermore, 1 Peter 3:7 calls husbands and wives' joint heirs of the grace of God.

In Proverbs chapter 31, the husband rises up and states that his wife excels all women (verse 29). In the same manner, the wife is to only talk about her husband to others with respect. Respect puts an end to nagging. Few things bother a man more than a nagging wife. Yes, I know that a husband who refuses to listen to his wife's input causes her frustration and she ends up nagging. However, realize women, that this does not work. Bringing grace into a marriage does. Colossians 4:6 encourages both husbands and wives to talk with grace. This verse alone can produce a heavenly marriage if we act on it.

Nothing beautifies a woman like submission. In 1 Peter 3:1-5, Peter notes the beauty of a submissive wife. I know many women do not like this word because it has been used too many times to oppress women. I will say again, submission is no longer submission when it is forced since biblical submission carries the thought of voluntary action. Take time to read the verses in 1 Peter noted above, and see that submission brings beauty to a woman like nothing else. In Genesis 20, the Bible notes that Sarah who called Abraham lord became so beautiful at 90 years of age that an ungodly king wanted her. And no, he was not blind.

In the same way, as nothing beautifies a woman more than submission, nothing exalts a man in a woman's eyes more than him submitting by loving her as Christ loves the church. I have to reiterate this point so that I am clear. Submission is for both wives and husbands. The husband who loves his wife as Christ loves the church is submitting to his wife but more importantly, to Jesus. If you have never heard this before just think about how God commands all of us to submit (see verse at the end). No matter what position or occupation a person has, they will always have someone or something to submit to. Even the President submits to the Constitution.

To summarize, submission is merely wives respecting their husbands and husbands loving their wives as Christ loves the church. Perhaps in no other area do I need to say it as in this area, **keep it simple.**

Key verse: 1 Peter 5:5-6, Yes, **all of you** (bold print mine) be submissive to one another and be clothed with humility for God resists the proud but gives grace to the humble. Therefore, humble yourselves (be submitted) under the mighty hand of God, that He may exalt you in due time, (parenthesis mine) …

THE LAW OF SOWING AND REAPING

I have often stated that the law of sowing and reaping makes marriage work. Alongside commitment, as stated in Step Five, this law makes marriage work. A law is something that works every time that it is put to work. What do you want out of your marriage? What do you want from your spouse? Well, plant it in them. In other words, do for them what you want them to do for you. You want your spouse to listen more? Then <u>you</u> do it.

In Galatians 6:7, Paul states that whatever a man sows that shall he also reap. Jesus stated in Luke 6:38 that as we give it would be given unto us. Sounds simple does it not? Many times, in speaking to Christians, I remind them that if we call ourselves Word people then let's apply the Bible in our marriages as we have been applying the two above-noted scriptures in our finances. Actually, a review of Luke 6:27-38 shows us that Jesus was talking about <u>all</u> aspects of our lives including finances.

So, let me ask again. What do you want from your spouse? Then plant it. If we believe Galatians 6:7 and Luke 6:38, then our faith response is to plant what we desire. Remember that Jesus stated (in our horizontal relationships with one another) that it is more blessed to give than to receive (Acts 20:35). This scripture alone can save a marriage. A word of caution, however. Do not plant just to get the other to do for you, but in honor to the Word, and if you do not quit the return will come. This is the promise in Galatians 6:9. You will reap if you do not quit.

Now read the scripture below with this in mind. Most of the time we read this scripture from a negative point of view. However, in the new covenant, this is a promise of good. Look up. You just found a great key to make your marriage heaven on the earth. If you do not feel like sowing remember what we have said about grace. Grace (unmerited favor) will empower you to sow, so lean on the grace, sow, and keep it simple.

Key verse: Galatians 6:7, Do not be deceived, God is not mocked; for whatever a man sows, that he will also reap.

BE COURTEOUS

This is actually a command in 1 Peter 3:8. But I have a question. Do you have to tell Christians and couples to be courteous? Well apparently, you do. Believe me when I tell you that simple courtesies such as "thank you" and "please" can go a long way in the marriage.

Alongside this truth, why not work on catching your spouse doing something good and acknowledging it? Couples usually have no problems catching one another doing something they do not like or reminding each other about something that they have failed to do. Do not let the terminal disease of taking your spouse for granted enter your marriage.

When a kind act is done, say "thank you." When you have a request, say "please." "Please" is a sign of honor, and we have already seen how important honor is to a marriage. So be courteous, be kind, and be gentle. Again, never leave a kind act in your marriage go unacknowledged. We will then be imitating God. Jesus stated that even giving someone a cup of water in His name would be rewarded by Him.

When your spouse does something that you assume is their responsibility to do for you (like cooking dinner or washing your car), say "thank you" anyway.

Men open the door for your wives. Never walk in public with her behind you. When calling one another on the phone, let the first words that come out of your mouth be "I love you" or at least "hi, sweetheart" then discuss what you need to talk about. Don't answer the phone saying things such as, "Yeah, what do you want?" Treat one another as you would treat a friend. Actually, your spouse should be your best friend (yes, I know after Jesus), so treat them even better than your friends. Greet one another when you get home from work. Say "good morning" and "good night," and keep it simple.

Key verse: I Peter 3:8, Finally, all of you be of one mind, having compassion for one another; love as brothers, be tenderhearted, be courteous.

WALK BY FAITH NOT BY SIGHT

When the Bible commands us to walk by faith and not by sight (2 Corinthians 5:7), it is telling us not to walk by our senses. We are not to walk by what we see, hear, taste or feel. Walking by faith in our marriages is one of the areas where our faith is tested the most. In fact, if we can walk by faith in our marriages, all other areas become easier.

It needs to be stated that the command to walk by faith is just that - a command. Also, we are to walk by faith means faith is to be a lifestyle, not just something we use when attacked or have a need. <u>In its simplest form walking by faith in your marriages is saying about your marriage what the Bible says about your marriage not what your physical senses tell you.</u> Faith framed the worlds according to Hebrews 11:3 and faith will frame your marriage. In fact, faith released by our words frames every area of our lives.

Let me ask you a big question. Are you walking by faith in your marriage? If you say you are, then I have to ask what Kenneth Hagin asked someone once who was believing

God in some area in their life, "What scriptures are you standing on?" The person replied to Brother Hagin "none in particular," and you have probably heard the answer he gave. He stated, "then that is what you will be getting - nothing in particular."

Find specific scriptures to stand on and declare them over your spouse and marriage. Declare the grace of God over your spouse and marriage. Wives can declare over their husbands that they love them as Christ loves the church. Husbands can declare what Solomon stated in Proverbs 31, that his wife does him good all the days of his life. Both need to declare that they have favor with one another. What are you declaring over your marriage every day? Are you declaring that your marriage is getting stronger or that it is doomed to fail? Remember the power in words.

Faith works when you put it to work. The Bible states that you have world overcoming faith in you (1 John 5:4). Your faith, if you do not quit, will lay hold of the heaven on earth you desire. Your faith will not make it happen, but faith is simply declaring what God has done (the finished work) or is doing now in your life. Yes, you can have the heavenly marriage you desire. Your faith and God's grace is the victory. As Brother Kenneth Hagin used to say, "Keep the switch of faith turned on." In the midst of a stand of faith, remember that God loves you, so do not quit. He is pulling for you. Speak the desired result over your spouse and marriage, not what you see in front of you. More on this later, so keep it simple.

Confession: I have world overcoming faith inside me because the Author and Finisher of my faith lives in me.

READ EPHESIANS 5:17-33 AND I CORINTHIANS 13:4-8 WEEKLY

My friends, nothing changes you like the Word. Counseling has its place, but nothing changes you like the Word in your heart. The Word of God is called the Word of His grace. As already stated, grace (God's unmerited favor) brings an empowerment, a strengthening. You do not have to succeed in marriage on your own. In fact, it cannot be done. God does not want you to even try it on your own. Read the above-noted verses every week but also spend time in the Word of God daily. It strengthens you, and by now you know that you need daily help to succeed in marriage. Spending time in the Word daily keeps it before your eyes. What we keep before our eyes, we will move toward.

Ultimately, what causes marriage to succeed is the development of the love of God in us. Reading the above scriptures regularly will do wonders in this area. Jesus stated that His words are spirit and life (John 6:63).

The verses noted above in Ephesians start with the imperatives to understand what the will of the Lord is (v.17) and to be filled with the Spirit (v.19). In being filled with the Spirit, we will understand the will of the Lord. We are filled with the Spirit (be-being filled in the Greek) by speaking to <u>ourselves</u> (KJV) in psalms, hymns, and spiritual songs. These are not necessarily songs from the hymnal, but divinely inspired utterances which may or may not be sung.

Here is the absolute key. It is in staying filled with the Spirit by these divine utterances (which come forth from our time with the Lord) that we can not only understand the will of the Lord but then submit to one another (v.21). In other words, we need to be being filled with the Spirit to submit to one another and for wives to submit and husbands to give themselves for their wives as Jesus gave Himself for us. A whole book can be written on this, but let's keep it simple.

I will give a word of caution in reading the scriptures from Ephesians 5. So many couples read this passage as an impossible admonition. Wives are told to submit and husbands to give their lives for their wives as Jesus gave Himself for us. However, these verses need to be read with this in mind. Husbands are not told to love their wives, but to love them <u>as they have been loved (Ephesians 5:25)</u>. A husband who knows and has received the love of God is now able to love his wife as Christ loves him. Wives are told to submit <u>as to the Lord</u> which means He is there to help her with her submission. In essence, the key is to read these verses as empowerments from the Lord. Jesus nourishes and cherishes us (Ephesians 5:29) so that we can become the husbands and wives He knows we can become.

In Ephesians chapter 5, we find the one thing she cannot do without and the one thing he cannot do without. At the risk of redundancy, affection is the wife's greatest need. This is the reason husbands are told in this passage to love their wives as Christ loves them. When a husband loves his wife as Christ loves the church, she will have no problem with submitting or respecting him. Selah. Husbands, stop and think about this. Husbands need to know respect (and submission) is never demanded but earned through loving their wives as Christ loved and loves them. This passage in Ephesians 5 notes that the husband washes his wife with words. Wives need daily washing from a myriad amount of negative thoughts.

Men cannot do without praise. Ephesians 5 again, calls it respect. Too much criticism, women, and a husband will feel that he cannot win with his wife. He will feel that he cannot make her happy and he will then quit.

In my opinion, the reason a woman needs words of affection is because most little girls do not grow up feeling loved, lovely and precious. Most men do not grow up feeling competent. You are free to disagree, of course, but why then would the Bible mention the need for affection and respect/praise as their greatest needs? Ephesians 5:26 is a key verse. In the Message Translation, it states, "Christ's love makes the church whole. His words evoke her beauty." As Christ's words to us, the husband's words are to evoke his wife's beauty. She will then feel loved, lovely and precious internally and externally. The same can be said for men. A wife will help her husband feel competent and honored by her words of praise.

1 Corinthians chapter 13 is the love chapter. It will change you and your marriage. Another word of instruction, however. If you have ever read 1 Corinthians 13, you already know that no one but Jesus has ever kept the instructions of this chapter all the time. Hence, no condemnation is allowed when you read this chapter. Thank God that when we cannot in our own efforts keep these instructions, Jesus can, and He lives in us. Actually, you can read this chapter as descriptive of Him and our Heavenly Father, and the love They have deposited in our hearts (Romans 5:5). This empowers us to love.

Therefore, stay in the Word. It creates faith and hope. Hope is positive expectancy. Hebrews 10:23 states not to let go of our hope. Do not lose hope or positive expectancy. Your marriage is getting better and better days are still to come. If we lose hope then we are hopeless, so do not lose it, and keep it simple.

Key verses: Proverbs 4:20-22, My son, give attention to my words; Incline your ear to my sayings. Do not let them depart from your eyes; Keep them in the midst of your heart; For they are life to those who find them, and health to all their flesh.

READ JOHN 8:1-12 REGULARLY

You may be asking what does this short story have to do with my marriage? The answer is everything. When you miss it in your marriage, be ready to apologize to one another and accept God's forgiveness of you. In this powerful but short story, Jesus did not condemn the woman. Yes, Pastor Samuel, but he told her not to do it again. No, He did not! I say it emphatically, He did not. He <u>empowered</u> her not to by not condemning her. See the difference? The gift of no condemnation empowered her.

I have said many times that I cannot tell even the godliest person in my church not to sin anymore. I am certain that the gift of no condemnation empowered her never to look for love in all the wrong places. Sounds like I heard these words before in a hymn somewhere. Just kidding.

Grace changed her, and it will change you and your marriage, so do not condemn yourself. Accept responsibility when you miss it but do not condemn yourself. Condemnation keeps us stuck, but <u>No Condemnation</u> (Romans 8:1) frees us to learn and grow. Remember, God loves you. His unmerited favor is there for us not because we do everything exactly right, but because we don't.

According to Hebrews 8:8-12, God can write in our hearts and minds as we believe the main clause of the new covenant, which is that He remembers our sins and iniquities no more. As we accept that we are forgiven, we can hear from the Lord steps to take when we miss it in our marriages. Is this an excuse to miss it in our marriages? No, since no real Christian is looking for excuses to miss it. However, many couples are looking for a way out of self-condemnation. Therefore, keep it simple like this chapter.

ADD GRACE TO YOUR MARRIAGE

I have talked about grace throughout this book. Again, grace is the undeserved and unmerited favor of God in our lives. Couples, we need to receive the grace of God in our individual lives and in our marriages daily. By now you realize that we need the grace of God to succeed in marriage. After being married for a short time, most couples find out marriage can be hard work. The temptation is then to either quit or work harder to make our marriage better. Actually, this is not keeping it simple. Grace is not trying to make things happen through our own self-efforts but relying on the favor of God. Is grace doing nothing? No, grace leads to Holy Spirit empowered activity rather than trying to make things happen in marriage. Trying to make things happen leads to working to change one another through nagging, fault finding, etc., etc.

The law of the old covenant demanded (the thou shalt not's) perfection, but grace supplies. John 1:17 states that the law was given through Moses, but grace and truth came through Jesus. Jesus brought grace because grace is a person—Jesus. Let's bring grace (Jesus) into our marriage. The law demanded perfection since the breaking of one law was, in essence, breaking them all. Grace gives unmerited, undeserved favor.

So why put your marriage under law by demanding from one another? Of course, requests made in love are always welcome in any marriage, but if we have a relationship with our spouse based on demands (or laws) we have put our marriage under law. Avoid demands and the "you are supposed to do this" or "you are supposed to do that for me" statements.

Let me reiterate, avoid demanding or expecting perfection from one another. Be gracious, be forgiving, give unmerited favor to one another, and empower your spouse to grow. Unless you have reached perfection in your marriage, give your spouse grace (favor) and bring The Blessing (Genesis 1:28) back to your marriage. Colossians 4:6 states that our speech should always be with grace. Ephesians 4:29 states to only speak that which ministers grace to others. A key verse is Romans 5:17. An abundance of grace is available to us in our marriages if we will learn to receive grace and give it to one another. This is a very powerful verse for our marriages once we understand what grace is. John 1:16 (AMPC) indicates that grace upon grace and favor upon favor has been heaped upon us through Jesus.

Let me mention again the need to <u>receive</u> grace from the Lord daily. Paul encouraged his son Timothy to be strong in the grace (2 Timothy 2:1). This simply means not relying on our own strength to do anything. Before his letters, the Apostle Paul always spoke grace to those He was writing to. He did this to encourage them to receive God's grace. We need it every day especially to be the husband or wife that God wants us to become. As I mentioned above, without receiving His grace we will try to make things happen in our marriages through our own self-efforts. Keep it simple by receiving and giving His grace, His undeserved and unmerited favor to one another every day.

Confession: I let no corrupt speech come out of my mouth, but only that which ministers God's undeserved and unmerited favor (grace). My speech is always with grace.

Father, I receive your grace today to be the husband (or wife) you have ordained me to be. I receive your grace, your undeserved, unmerited favor into my marriage. I rely on your help and intervention. I declare your grace today over my spouse and our marriage, in Jesus' name.

DATE

Yes, date. Simple isn't it. However, most couples do not date. Oh, I am not saying that they do not go out. Dating involves two things that couples used to do when dating. After marriage, for the most part, couples don't do these two things anymore.

Dating involves, first of all setting a date. That is, setting a day and time in advance. As much as I appreciate spontaneity in marriages, most couples in our fast-paced society need to set a date and time in advance.

Secondly, is the preparation. Here, I am not just talking about getting a babysitter in advance or calling the restaurant for reservations. I am talking about getting yourself ready emotionally and physically for your time with the most important person in your life. Of course, husbands need to be aware that a stay-at-home mom does not have all the time to get herself ready that she did when she was single. Husbands (or wives) may now have a job that at times keeps them in the office late. It is good to just do the best you can with the time one has.

Let me give you an example of preparation. The husband or wife should not accept if at all possible, a phone call at the last minute at work knowing that they need to leave right on time to get home and get ready. The husband may need to get home on time to help his wife with getting the little ones to the sitter. And both need to be emotionally present when they go out. I personally do not want to have anything on my mind when it is date time. I want to be present to enjoy my time with her.

Please do not take anything I say as rigid law. If spontaneity works best in your marriage, then go for it. On the flip side of this, do not avoid time with one another every day rationalizing that in a few days it is date night and you will have more time with one another. Therefore, dating does not mean ignoring each other until the date night. The date night just adds to what couples should be doing all the time and that is spending time with each other. I am just talking to those couples who can get so busy with both working, the five kids, two dogs, three cats, T-ball, soccer, PTA, Zumba, and even church that they need to set a day to get away by themselves.

Along these same lines, whenever possible, I recommend couples take a weekend alone and out of town once or twice a year. No children allowed in the weekend away. Make it two nights away or at least one and keep it simple by avoiding too many activities and the TV, computer and cell phones. Smile, couples.

Key verses: Song of Solomon 2:13b and 7:11,12b, Rise up, my love, my fair one, and come away! Come, my beloved, let us go forth to the field; Let us lodge in the villages. There I will give you my love.

CAST OUT ALL FEAR

All fear in marriage and in all areas of our lives must be cast out. I say all areas of our lives because fear in any area of our lives will affect our marriage. For example, if the husband fears lack then when his wife appears to be overspending, his fear will bring conflict to the relationship. There are no healthy fears. I respect dogs especially those I do not know but do not fear them. No fear is good because God has not given us a spirit of fear as shown in 2 Timothy 1:7.

Do not allow fear to be a motivator in your life. The man who fears poverty and lack because he grew up with it may discipline himself to work hard to achieve a high level of success so as to never worry about money. However, the fear will still be in him; hence, he will never really enjoy his success. His fear is compounded by fearing he could lose his level of success.

Fear prevents couples from discussing sexual issues. It is interesting that we commit to one another for life, but fear discussing with our spouse our fears, dreams and needs. Why? It is because we fear being misunderstood and rejection. A serious issue is that where the absence of <u>fright</u> exists, we think fear is not there. We only become aware of a fear when panic or something along those lines occurs. The devil is happy when we are not even aware of the fears we bring into our marriages.

In keeping with step one, nothing casts out fear like a revelation that God loves you. Please do not read quickly over this step. Remember that the Holy Spirit was sent to teach us all things even how to overcome fear in all areas of our lives. 1 John 4:16-18 shows us that God loves us, that fear is torment, and that perfected love (Jesus Himself-the revelation that He loves us) casts it out of our lives.

Let me summarize a few steps in overcoming fear. Develop faith in God's love for you. Speak to fear when you recognize its presence. Tell it to leave in the name of Jesus. Live a life of forgiveness and love. If you miss it, do not condemn yourself, just receive your forgiveness (Colossians 2:13, 1 John 2:12). Remember that God has promised never to leave us (Hebrews 13:5-6). And remember that you have been delivered from fear (Hebrews 2:14-15). No, I do not believe you will have to go to therapy for a year. Just believe the love, keep hearing messages on the love of God, and keep it simple.

Key verses: 1 John 4:16 and 18, And we have known and believed the love God has for us. God is love, and he who abides in love abides in God, and God in him. There is no fear in love; but perfect love casts out fear.

SEX

OK, now that fear is cast out, we can discuss sex. Years ago, the Lord revealed something that is essential in the sexual relationship. It is that women generally desire sex when they feel connected emotionally to their husbands. Men desire sex not just for the obvious physical benefits but to feel close to their wives. Do you see the difference? Women are more inclined to have (and enjoy sex) when they feel connected. Men are more desirous of sex due to the obvious physical aspects of sex but also to feel connected to their wives. If interested you can explore articles by Dr. Juli Slattery on the Focus on the Family website (or her website authenticintimacy.com) that verify what I have known for years, that sex is an emotional, spiritual and relational need for men.

Men need to connect with their wives by listening to them when they get home. They should help clean the kitchen, assist with the children or do whatever it is that makes her feel loved. Remember her daily need for affection. Of course, men, do not do these things simply because at night you will request sex. Women recognize that sex is not just a physical thing with men in spite of what the media presents in movies and TV shows.

The best thing couples can do to improve their sex lives is to talk about sex. This is so obvious, but couples fear talking. It is important to remember here that sex was God's idea to begin with. Hollywood did not invent sex. They just exploit it for commercial purposes. There are many good books by Christians that you can read to learn more about sex. I am not against any of them, but, couples, realize that you have two sex manuals at home. The first one is called the Bible, specifically, the book Song of Solomon. The other sex manual is one another. Therefore, talk about what is desired and what is not desired. Discuss what is pleasurable and what is not. And never push your spouse to do something they are not comfortable doing.

Couples recognize when you have brought unhealthy notions to the marriage from sex being at worse disgusting and at best something to be tolerated. Ask the Holy Spirit to help you identify any unbiblical beliefs you may have about sex. And (are you ready for this?) ask God to help you develop your sex life.

And finally, putting all the other aspects of this book alongside this chapter, your priority in sex is not to get your needs met but your spouse's. However, this does not mean you should feel guilty of wanting to or even enjoying sex.

Enjoy one another. This is part of the abundant life Jesus came to bring us (John 10:10). In 1 Timothy 6:17 the Apostle Paul indicates that God has given us all things (including sex) to enjoy. Enjoy God's gift of sex for marriage and keep it simple.

Key Verse: Song of Solomon 1:2, Let him kiss me with the kisses of his mouth--For your love is better than wine.

STEP TWENTY-THREE

TALK

In the last step, I discussed the importance of talking. So, let's talk about talking. Men generally talk to transact business. Women talk to talk. In other words, they talk because they enjoy talking. Women enjoy talking to connect with others. Can you see the issue here? Husband gets home to relax, and the wife asks, "Honey can we talk?" You have heard this before. Husband says, "About what?" He figures the bills are paid, there is plenty of money in the bank, the kids are doing well, and I got her car serviced last week. There is nothing to talk about.

Men recognize that women talk for talking's sake. They feel emotionally connected to their husbands when they can talk. Besides, men, women need to talk when they are overwhelmed by situations. Men generally stuff things, but women like to and need to release built-up emotions. Men need to do the same, but generally do not admit it.

You may have heard it said that women talk several thousand more words per day than men. However, this has not been scientifically proven. In the interest of keeping it simple, I merely point to the known fact that women like their men to talk. Men generally do not see the value in talking when there are other things to do when they get home. However, both men and women (but especially men) need to see talking on a daily basis as an indispensable part of keeping all the other steps of this book active.

Let me give you some simple tips. Set up a time before going to bed for talking. Maybe after dinner when the children are in bed. When a man knows that a certain time is set aside for talking, he will not feel threatened when the wife asks, "Honey, can we talk?" If this does not work for you, then give each other permission to say, "Honey, can we talk about this at such and such a time, so I can give you my undivided attention?" In other words, your daily time may be at a different hour every day but talking will occur every day. I also believe in using the opportunities that arise throughout the day. Look for them. It may be a few minutes at a time. Do what works.

Just like we cannot have a relationship with our Savior without talking to Him every day we cannot have a relationship with each other if we do not talk. In its simplest form, talking draws people closer, while not talking draws people apart. Men, you need your wife to talk. You need to know how she is doing. And she needs to know how you are doing. Learn to talk more to your spouse than anyone else and when the other is talking listen and keep it simple.

Key Verse: Proverbs 16:24, Pleasant words are like a honeycomb, Sweetness to the soul and health to the bones.

LISTEN

This step is not as hard as we make it. The problem is that we were not taught to listen by our parents. Oh yes, they insisted we listen to them, our teachers and all in authority, but generally we were not taught the fine art of listening. In many homes, the fine art of interrupting was taught. Dad interrupted mom, mom interrupted dad, both parents interrupted the kids, and when grandma and grandpa came over it, was a free for all of interruptions.

Listening, real listening, involves shutting the mouth and opening the ears. It also involves suspending all judgments while the other is talking. We also need to hear not just the content but the heart of the person talking.

Jesus is the Great Listener. He stated in Matthew 13:15 that when we <u>hear,</u> then <u>understanding</u> comes. My <u>thoughts</u> (toward my spouse, for example) change and <u>healing</u> comes. Wow, what a simple pattern of what happens when we finally hear our spouse. I <u>listen and</u> begin to <u>understand</u> why they do something or hold a certain belief; hence, I change (NKJV uses the word turn) my beliefs or <u>thoughts</u> toward my spouse. This then brings <u>healing</u> to the relationship. So what Jesus was endeavoring to get us to understand is that listening brings healing. As we listen to Him and the Bible, healing comes to us. This works in marriage. As we listen to one another, healing comes to the relationship.

Simple isn't it. I do not listen to prepare my counter-argument, but for understanding. In other words, I am not an attorney preparing my counter-argument. Someone stated that I should seek to understand rather than to be understood. Another pointed out the obvious that since God gave us two ears and one mouth, we need to do twice the amount of listening than talking. And learn to give feedback to one another to see if, in fact, you understood. If you did not, then the other can clarify their communication further. In true listening, we are not trying to convince the other of our point of view. We are simply trying to understand the other. James said it best in the Bible quote below so listen, listen, listen and keep it simple.

Key verse: James 1:19, Therefore, my beloved brethren, let every man be swift to hear, slow to speak, slow to wrath.

WISDOM-THE PRINCIPAL THING/ PRAYING FOR ONE ANOTHER

Proverbs 4:7 states that wisdom is the principal thing. Therefore, it is obvious that couples need to pray for wisdom to be the spouse God desires them to be. Wisdom helps us say the right things at the right time, dictates to us when to keep our mouths closed and when to pick our fights. Wisdom is the foundation for all the steps along with our personal relationship with Jesus as noted in the introduction.

Wisdom leads us to pray for one another. I do not believe that couples have to spend all their prayer time praying together since couples generally have different things to pray for. My wife and I both pray for our son every day and the leaders of our country, but as a pastor to my church and as a pastor to other pastors, I have different things to pray about. However, we do pray together regularly.

Pray for God to give wisdom to your spouse and not just as it relates to your relationship with each other, but that God will give your spouse wisdom in all areas of their lives.

Colossians 1:9 is a good verse to pray. Do not pray that God will straighten them out or show them where they are not meeting your needs. Pray the Word. Other verses to pray are the prayers of Paul in Ephesians chapters 1 and 3.

Pray and speak Bible verses over one another. Wives, instead of complaining to God about your husband, declare that they love you as Christ loves the church. Husbands, instead of complaining that your wives do not respect you, declare that they respect you as stated in Ephesians chapter 5. Now you see part of the reason I encouraged you to read the passage in Ephesians chapter 5 every week. As you read it every week, it is in front of you to do it and to speak these verses over one another.

I have heard wives bemoan the fact that their husbands do not take spiritual leadership in the home. Therefore, wives, declare that they <u>are</u> the leaders in the home God desires them to be. Declare that they have a revelation of how much God loves them. Actually, both can declare by faith that the eyes of the understanding of their spouse is enlightened to God's love for them. Nothing will transform our spouse more than a revelation of God's love. Husbands can go to Proverbs chapter 31 and declare verses from that chapter over your wives.

This is doing Romans 4:17, speaking things that do not exist as though they did. This is how God talks. God never speaks the problem, but the desired end result. You can either speak what you already have or speak what you desire to have. And remember that according to Matthew 18:19, agreement in prayer is powerful. The greatest agreement in prayer is between a husband and a wife.

Here is the simple issue here. You can complain, or you can pray and speak God's Word over one another. Complaining accomplishes nothing. And finally, pray that God will give you favor with your spouse, that He will help you look upon them with favor and help you see them as He does. I heard a great man of God say once that if Jesus was able to turn the water into wine, then he can turn the water of our marriages into intoxicating wine. We just have to ask. Pray, speak God's Word, and keep it simple.

Key verse: Proverbs 15:8b, But the prayer of the upright is His delight.

DO NOT GIVE OFFENSE

In 1 Corinthians 10:32, the Apostle Paul admonishes us to give no offense to the Jews, unbelievers or to Christians. Maybe he should have specifically added to give no offense to wives and husbands. I know that in marriage we must be quick to forgive, but that is another step. This step is not to offend. Yes, I know offenses will come even in the best of marriages but keep reading.

Years ago, I found out it bothered my wife when I used her car and did not leave the keys where I had found them. Now do not refer me back to Step Eleven where I discussed not to major on the minors. I simply learned to leave the keys where I found them to not cause offense to the person, I love the most in the world (other than Jesus).

After being married even a few days, couples start finding out what bothers their spouse. I am not implying that everyone walks around on tiptoes so as not to offend one another. And I am also not saying to get into fear that you will offend the other one. I am simply saying as a person told me once, when you know where the mines are in the river, drive around them.

I previously talked to men about accepting responsibility for issues or conflicts that come up in the marriage. Here I want to encourage both spouses to eliminate the blame game (started with Adam and Eve) and be quick to judge themselves for their part whenever conflicts occur. The truth is that the more I know God loves me and the more I know my sins are forgiven (Ephesians 1:7, Colossians 2:13), the quicker I can ask for forgiveness from my spouse and judge myself. No, I am not talking about condemning myself only accepting responsibility where I was wrong.

I heard that someone famous was asked once who should be the first one in a marital conflict to apologize. His answer was classic. He stated, "The one who was in the right." Selah, pause and think about it.

Enough said. Now go to the next chapter and keep it simple.

Key verse: Romans 14:13, Therefore let us not judge one another anymore, but rather resolve this, not to put a stumbling block or a cause to fall in our brother's way.

DO NOT TAKE OFFENSE

So now that we have covered the previous step, we can discuss this one. Years ago, when I was teaching a class on Anger Management, I stated that Martinez's first law of anger management was not to take anything personally. Stay with me on this one because this does not mean we do not take it to heart when our spouse is upset. Good listening is needed there.

Here I am talking about not getting offended every time we are corrected. Yes, I remember step eleven on not making minor issues major ones. I wrote it. We are not to be picky over small issues, but at the same time when corrected, why not say, "Thank you for telling me," instead of taking everything personally and getting into a big discussion.

Some couples make an issue every time the other shares a concern in the home. "You forgot to feed Spot," (Chico in my home) becomes "Are you trying to tell me I am not taking care of the dog? YOU forgot to feed the cat last week, too." Wow! All the spouse said was "you forgot to feed the dog." Yes, I know that since you have been reading this book, you know your spouse could have said "the dog was not fed this morning" rather than "YOU did not feed the dog." But, alas, we are still learning, so take no offense. Take nothing personally.

And even if your spouse <u>was</u> rude, you can still decide not to get offended. I am not saying that you may not bring up later what they said or did. I am just pointing out that many times we just need to forgive and not bring it up again. Listen to what the Holy Spirit tells you to do. Many times, I simply hear Him tell me to drop it and take no offense. Actually, the more we understand our completeness in Christ, and how much Jesus loves us the less we will take offense. Hence, keep it simple.

Key verse: Ephesians 4:32, And be kind to one another, tenderhearted, forgiving one another, even as God in Christ forgave you.

DO THINGS TOGETHER/HAVE TIME APART

Remember the old saying about the family that prays together, staying together. It is not just in praying together, but in doing <u>anything</u> good together. That is why dating as already indicated is so important. My wife and I (as most couples) do not enjoys the same things. She does not enjoy riding the bike to the beach. She likes driving the car. Therefore, find things you can do together. Do not tell me that there is nothing you both enjoy doing together. You can learn to enjoy doing things together. Where one enjoys walking on the beach and the other likes to swim in the ocean, take time switching activities. One day do what he enjoys and the next week what she enjoys. A word of caution, couples. Do not <u>tolerate</u> the activity your spouse enjoys. Learn to enjoy it.

On the other side of the spectrum give each other time to be alone. I enjoy time at home alone reading a good book. My wife enjoys going to the gym. When she does, I can take a long bike ride. Couples should not insist that all of their time be spent together. However, for me, time with my wife is still the priority and not time with my male friends. This step should not be interpreted to mean that frequent long trips out of town by oneself are healthy. The more time we spend together, the less temptation there is.

The verse below is specifically talking about the sexual relationship, but it applies to anytime together, so keep it simple.

Key verse: 1 Corinthians 7:5, Do not deprive one another except with consent for a time, ... and come together again...

THE CHILDREN

Into most marriages, children will come. Children can add stress to any marriage, but they do not have to destroy it. Actually, if we do it right, children will make our marriages better. Therefore, let me give you a few simple tips. Read the Bible and find out what it states on parenting. Ask your pastor to recommend a good Christian book on parenting. I do recommend my upcoming book *Amazing Parenting*. There are many good books on parenting, but make sure they are biblically based.

Come to an agreement on how you will discipline the children, on who will help with homework, who will teach what to them, etc., etc. It will help that you have already read the step on talking. A lot of talking will be needed here.

Couples need to talk out all the parenting issues and plan ahead, because as the children grow new situations will spring up. It is good to talk, for example, on how to handle dating in the home when our girls and boys get to the teenage years. At what age will we allow dating? <u>Will</u> we allow dating? What does the Bible say? In other words, talk about issues years ahead of time and find out what the Bible, the best parenting book, says.

Have communion as a family regularly. Additionally, have regular time with your children around the Bible. With our younger children, particularly, reading Bible stories is very important. The most important part is the example we give to our children. Let them see you valuing the Bible and see prayer as fellowship with God rather than as a religious duty. Teach them by your example that going to church is honoring God and expressing our thanks and not something we do because we HAVE to.

Remember that your children will parent much the same way they are parented. Hence, let me give you a few tips. Take caution correcting one another's parenting in front of the children. If it has to be done do it respectfully. And never talk about your spouse disparagingly in front of the children.

Parenting takes time. One of the first things children need is two parents actively involved in their lives. Men be involved in your children's lives. The greatest thing we give our children is a correct image of who God is. If a father is absent, (physically but also emotionally), that is how children will see God, as uncaring and absent. Many of the things in this book apply to parenting. Be courteous to them. Find something to praise them about every day. Children are word-made. Add grace to your parenting. Listen. Take them out. Speak God's word over them and tell them every day God and you love them. Children cannot live without words and meaningful touch on a daily basis. Children's sense of value (or lack of it) comes from how we parented them.

Couples let your children hear you compliment one another. Be affectionate with each other in front of them and let them see that you enjoy doing things together. And, yes, discipline is part of parenting, but discipline must be founded on the relationship that you have built with them. In my book on parenting, I advise parents that the most important thing we desire from our children is to develop a relationship with them. From the relationship obedience to us will flow.

Do not misunderstand me. Building a relationship with them is not becoming their best friend. Building a relationship with them is communicating your love to them daily, listening and taking time daily with them. Children who feel loved, obey. Yes, there can be exceptions, but if parents continue to love, they will come around. As Paul stated in Romans 2:4, the goodness of God leads people and our children to repentance.

Parenting is a very noble and important task that is not valued as in past generations. And yet, your relationship with your spouse is still first. Parenting was never intended by God to be difficult. Just work together, believe God for His grace and wisdom to parent. As you are not alone in your marriage, you are not alone in bringing up your children. God is with and for us, so lean on His help and the Bible and keep it simple.

Remember the R-R-R rule: Rules with no Relationship brings Rebellion.

HAVE A VISION FOR YOUR MARRIAGE

L
et me ask you a question. Do you have a vision for your marriage and do you have it written down? Now that you have read most of this book you are ready to dream and write. A vision is a dream, an expectation, a goal.

After you write it down, it is good to keep it in front of you by reading it weekly. Additionally, declare that you already have it by faith. A word of caution, however. Your vision should not state that you dream of someday your husband (or wife) changing and loving you unconditionally. That statement is one-sided and selfish. Your vision should sound something like the following:

My vision for my marriage is to have us communicate in love and respect. To have a marriage where we are committed to working through our differences no matter what. A marriage where our commitment to one another and our love for one another will grow stronger and stronger as the years go by. A marriage where we are both committed to helping one another to accomplish the call of God on our lives. A marriage where our children will see the Biblical model for marriage demonstrated in front of them, and where in our later years we will be a role model to younger couples. A marriage where we will leave a legacy for the glory of God. When we are gone, people and our children will still remember what we taught them about marriage and lived out in front of them.

Proverbs 19:18 (KJV) states that without a vision, people will perish. People perish when they have no positive expectation of life getting better. In marriage, people perish when they stop expecting their marriage to get better. Hope (positive expectation or your vision) delayed or deferred makes the heart sick (Proverbs 13:12). When written down it becomes clearer and clearer, and expectation rises especially when we keep it in front of us. Couples need to work together using the steps in this book to develop their vision and declare it done by faith. The book of Habakkuk encourages us by stating that the vision will surely come to pass (Habakkuk 2:3). Write the vision and keep it simple.

Key verse: Habakkuk 2:2, ...Write the vision and make it plain...

LEAVE AND CLEAVE

My parents were from Mexico, and in that nation, many newlyweds still move in with the in-laws. But the Bible clearly admonishes us against it. Actually, the admonishment is specifically to the men.

It is important not just to leave physically, but emotionally as well. When I married, I became my wife's husband first, and was now my mother's son second. I was to be more concerned with her needs and desires than those of my mother's. What mom or dad felt about a decision concerning my marriage was of secondary importance to how my wife felt. I still respected my parents, but my wife was the priority and developing our home was the important thing.

What about the cleaving part? This part has to do with all that has already been stated in the previous chapters. However, the cleaving part also has to do with divorce. Divorce is not an option. Yes, I know that divorce does occur even in many Christian homes. And divorce is not the unpardonable sin, contrary to what some legalistic people think. There are times when a spouse needs to leave such as in the case of domestic violence. Do not let the devil condemn you if you have gone through a divorce.

However, here is my point. Far too many couples are entering marriage with the mindset that if it does not work out, then they can divorce. I believe that couples need to enter marriage with the thought that since God is for them, with His help, they will succeed and teach others how to win in marriage as well. If you have to get help from your pastor or a Christian counselor, then do it. My friends, you can succeed in marriage. Just lean on His grace, follow the biblical model for marriage, and keep it simple.

Key verse: Genesis 2:24, Therefore a man will leave his father and mother and be joined (cleave) to his wife, and they shall become one flesh.

Philippians 2:13, For it is God who works in you both to will and to do for His good pleasure.

FINAL THOUGHTS

As I close this book, I want to encourage you again that you are not alone. When I married, I determined not to duplicate my parents' marriage, but without the knowledge of the Bible, I did. For years, I struggled with guilt over this. My point is that when we realize that God is on our side and wants good things for us, the struggle stops. I was trying to do things on my own without His help. Don't do that as this is a major point in this book. The Apostle Paul went as far as to say that when he did not know what to do in a certain situation, he was not being weak but strong since now he had to rely on the grace of our Lord (2 Corinthians 12:10).

Paul stated that God is for us (Romans 8:31). David added that God is on our side (Psalm 118:6). My friend, you are not alone. Go to His Word and apply it in your life. Never forget that He invented marriage and wants your marriage to be heaven on earth more than you do.

Remember that it is more blessed to give than receive (Acts 20:32). When it comes to our relationship with our Heavenly Father, He is more interested that we come to receive from Him. However, in our horizontal relationships, it is more blessed to give than to receive. In marriage, we need to apply this more than in any area of our lives. More blessed to give. The word blessed means empowered. Empowerment is released into your marriage when one spouse or the other believes this verse and decides to be the initiator of giving.

Rely on the Holy Spirit. He is your Helper. He has been sent to teach us all things and guide us into all truth. The Holy Spirit knows everything about marriage. See John 14:26 and John 16:13 as verses applying to your marriage. Ask Him for help in making decisions and in all marital discussions. The Holy Spirit will also help you in saying the right things to your spouse, when to broach a difficult subject, and even alerts us when issues are going on with our spouse. We need His help. The Holy Spirit is there to lead us in our marriages as Paul stated in Romans 8:14. Most marriage seminars fail even to mention the need to rely on and ask the Holy Spirit for His help in our relationships.

Contend for your marriage. It will be worth the effort, especially as you see change and your marriage becomes a praise to the Lord. We do not wrestle against flesh and blood. Your spouse is not the real problem. The devil is, so cast him out and keep speaking the word of God over your marriage and leaning on the grace of God.

The Lord bless you and keep you. The Lord make His face shine upon your marriage, favor you, lift up His countenance upon you, and grant you peace. I speak peace to your marriage – nothing missing, nothing broken. I declare your marriage blessed and that the best years of your marriage are ahead of you. Thanks for keeping it simple.

AN INVITATION

Congratulations on finishing. If you have never invited Jesus Christ to be your Lord and Savior, I want personally to give you the invitation to do so. I have explained some principles of Jesus, but now want to give you an invitation to receive Him. The principles alone will not help you without the person of Jesus. The Bible makes it very easy to invite Him into your life and marriage. The book of Romans states that if we believe in our hearts that God raised Jesus from the dead and with our mouths declare Him Lord, you will be born again.

This is not changing churches or even joining one. It is simply accepting the free gift that Jesus purchased for you when the Bible states He died to pay for all mankind's sin. This is when life really begins, for when we accept the free gift, God has a legal right to move into our spirits and cause them to be born again. God, Himself, becomes our Father. God moves in to live with you to guide you and help you.

Simply pray a simple prayer such as this: Dear God, I believe Jesus died for me and was raised from the dead. I receive Him as my Lord and Savior. That is all there is to it. Jesus did the hard part. Keep it simple.

Write to me if you need to find a church. If you know a Bible teaching church, join it. Start reading His Word, the Bible, and finding out how much He loves you. You are now His child. Congratulations!

VERSES ON MARRIAGE

Genesis 2:18, And the Lord God said, "It is not good for the man to be alone; I will make him a helper comparable to him."

Genesis 8:22, "While the earth remains Seedtime and harvest, shall not cease."

Proverbs 18:22, "He who finds a wife finds a good thing and obtains favor from the Lord."

Ephesians 5:25, "Husbands, love your wives, as Christ also loved the church and gave Himself for her."

Ephesians 5:33, "Nevertheless let each one of you in particular so love his own wife as himself, and let the wife see that she respects her husband."

Luke 6:38, "Give, and it will be given to you:"

Colossians 3:18-19, "Wives, submit to your own husbands, as is fitting in the Lord. Husbands, love your wives and do not be bitter toward them."

1 Peter 3:1, 6, "Wives, likewise, be submissive to your own husbands, that even if some do not obey the Word, they, without a word, may be won by the conduct of their wives, v.6 as Sarah obeyed Abraham, calling him lord, whose daughters you are if you do good and are not afraid with any terror."

1 Peter 3:7, "Husbands, likewise, dwell with them with understanding, giving honor to the wife, as to the weaker vessel, and as being heirs together of the grace of life, that your prayer may be not hindered."

I John 5:4, "For whatever is born of God overcomes the world. And this is the victory that has overcome the world – our faith."

Mark 11:24, "Therefore, I say to you, whatever things you ask when you pray, believe that you receive them, and you will have them."

Psalm 37:4, "Delight yourself also in the Lord, And He shall give you the desires of your heart."

FAMOUS SAYINGS ON MARRIAGE

To keep your marriage brimming, with love in the loving cup, whenever you're wrong, admit it; whenever you are right, shut up. - Ogden Nash

Keep your eyes wide open before marriage, and half shut afterward. – Ben Franklin

If you want to know how something works, talk to the person who made it. - Creflo Dollar

To have a happy home, you both must develop the habit of walking in the Love of God. - Gloria Copeland

A husband and wife will see things differently, but if they are both committed to the Word, strife can't exist. - Kenneth Copeland

Happy marriage begins when we marry the ones we love, and they blossom when we love the ones we marry. - Terry Mullen

No one knows what perfect love is until they have been married a quarter of a century - Mark Twain

Marriage is our last best chance to grow up. – Joseph Barth

Let the wife make the husband glad to come home and let him make her sorry to have him leave. – Martin Luther

The highest level of love is loving as a decision. – Kenneth Copeland

Marriage is like when you love someone and give them a ring. – Gigi Patino, my great niece when she was four years old

ABOUT THE AUTHOR:

Samuel Martinez pastors Amazing Love Ministries, a church with English and Spanish services. FCF is part of the FCF fellowship of churches. He loves to teach on the goodness and the love of God. He was ordained in 1986 and has a master's degree in Marriage, Family and Child Counseling. Prior to beginning full-time ministry in 2001 he worked in the counseling field. He has taught parenting classes for over 25 years and has been married for over 48 years.

He can be reached by e-mail at <u>Smartinez@cfaith.com</u> or by regular mail at Amazing Love Ministries, <u>216 S Citrus</u> P O Box 503 West Covina Calif. 91791

Made in the USA
Lexington, KY
21 November 2019